Greek Sacred Sites

EPIDAURUS
CENTRE OF HEALING

JILL DUDLEY

PUT IT IN YOUR POCKET SERIES
ORPINGTON PUBLISHERS

Published by
Orpington Publishers

Cover design and origination by
Creeds, Bridport, Dorset
01308 423411

Printed and bound in the UK by
Creeds

© Jill Dudley 2016

ISBN: 978-0-9935378-6-8

EPIDAURUS
CENTRE OF HEALING

In antiquity Epidaurus was once the most important centre for the worship of Asclepius, god of medicine. Situated amongst pine trees in the north-east of the Peloponnese, it is surrounded by distant mountains which cradle the visitor, giving him a sense of security, peace and well-being.

Before Asclepius took over this sanctuary, his father Apollo (also a god of medicine, but more famed for prophecy, archery and music), was worshipped at a temple on the nearby summit of Mount Kynortion in the seventh century B.C.

There were several stories regarding the birth of Asclepius, all somewhat strange ones. The first was that a mortal beauty, whose name was Coronis, was once loved by Apollo. After Coronis became pregnant by him she was unfaithful, and Apollo was told of it by a white crow (at that time all crows were white); he was so enraged by Coronis' infidelity that he killed her, although some say it was his devoted twin sister, the goddess Artemis, who did this in order to avenge the insult to her brother. Afterwards, however, Apollo was filled with such remorse, he took it out on the crow for informing against her, and put a curse on the bird, turning it black, since when all crows have been black.

It is said that Apollo rescued the baby Asclepius from the

body of Coronis, and entrusted the child to the wise Chiron, a centaur who was half-man, half-horse. Chiron lived in a cave on Mount Pelion in Thessaly in north-east Greece, and was renowned throughout the ancient world for his wisdom, medical knowledge, his music and his justice.

A second story has Coronis pregnant by Apollo, but giving birth to Asclepius at Epidaurus where she exposes him on a mountainside. There the infant is guarded by a sheepdog, and suckled by a goat. When the owner misses his two animals, he goes in search of them and finds them caring for the baby; he immediately recognizes the child's divinity by the light that shines about him, and takes him home. Later, the child is put in the care of Chiron from whom he receives his education.

A third story makes Asclepius the son of quite a different woman named Arsinoe. According to Pausanias, a second century A.D. travel-writer, an enquirer went to Delphi* to find out if Arsinoe was his real mother and was told conclusively by the Pythia (Apollo's priestess and spokeswoman) that Asclepius' mother was Coronis. Apollo's answer was as follows:

O Asklepios
shoot of universal joy,
whom Phlegyas's daughter bore to me,
beautiful Koronis
with whom I mingled
in love in rocky Epidaurus.

The present Epidaurus centre was founded in the sixth century B.C., and quickly became renowned throughout the world for its miraculous healing powers. The centre's aim was to heal not just the afflicted part of the body, but mind and spirit also, hence its theatre, stadium and gymnasium (the latter two sadly now only ruins).

A Panhellenic festival, the Asclepieia, was founded in the fifth century B.C. in honour of the god. This was held every four years, and consisted of events such as athletics, chariot races, music and poetry. Plato, the great fourth century B.C. philosopher, mentioned a man named Ion who boasted he had won first prize for his recital of Homer's *Iliad* at the Asclepieia.

Asclepius was said to have married a woman named Epione by whom he had two sons, Machaon and Podalirius, both of whom were mentioned in the *Iliad* as they had fought with the Greeks in the Trojan War, and tended the wounded on the battlefield. Two of Asclepius' daughters had interesting names – Hygiea (from where our word 'hygiene' comes), and Panacea (meaning 'universal remedy').

It is the wonderfully preserved theatre at Epidaurus, dating from 330 B.C., which is the greatest attraction at the site today. It is built into the natural contour of the hillside, and is famed for its acoustics. From the small round marble altar to Dionysos, god of wine and drama, in the centre of the orchestra (where the chorus in a drama danced and sang), the most hushed whisper, or the tearing of a scrap of paper, or dropping of a tiny coin can be heard clearly from the highest seats. Originally it had a seating capacity for six thousand people, but was then extended to take thirteen thousand. It has fifty-one tiers, each tier reached by a number of steep-stepped aisles fanning outwards from the orchestra below. It was up behind this theatre that the earlier temple of Apollo had been.

In antiquity, those not arriving overland to Epidaurus would have sailed in to the ancient port of Palea Epidaurus. On arrival they would have followed the Sacred Way and entered through the great *propylaea* (the entrance to the temenos, the sacred enclosure). Following the processional way they would have come to the temple of Asclepius at the heart of the temenos. This marked the site where it was believed the god had been born. The temple was thirty-four metres long, and was graced with numerous columns, its pediment being of white Pentelic marble.

In the *cella* of the temple (the most sacred inner room) there would have been the gold and ivory cult statue of Asclepius seated on a throne and holding his habitual staff on which was a coiled snake. Asclepius was always depicted, in art or on pottery, wearing a *himation* (a cloak with the right end thrown over the left shoulder), and holding his staff with the coiled snake on it. Beside his cult statue was a dog – dogs were sacred to him, no doubt because at birth he had been guarded by a dog when exposed on the mountainside. And maybe it was the myth of the birth of Asclepius and the death of his mother, that caused it to become the rule that no one was allowed entry to this sacred site who was on the point of giving birth or dying.

In the vicinity of the temple was the *abaton*, a columned stoa where invalids, after ritual purification and sacrifice, would spend the night hoping by morning to find themselves cured through divine intervention; some were advised in a dream what remedy or medication was necessary to aid their recovery.

In the *abaton* were Asclepius' sacred snakes. They were

yellowish in colour, and would slither up and lick a patient's festering wound or skin complaint and so effect a cure. In those days snakes were not considered sinister and evil, but were symbolic of divine wisdom. Certainly there at this centre of healing, snakes were sacred and beneficial. They were even brought from Epidaurus to other Asclepeion sanctuaries, one of which was on the island of Kos* where the fifth century B.C. Hippocrates, father of western medicine, lived and worked, and where his father was a priest-physician at the temple of Asclepius.

Numerous valuable votive offerings have been found at Epidaurus, given in gratitude by patients. There were also stelae inscribed with miraculous recoveries: a dumb child, for instance, who, after a night in the *abaton,* was able to speak; someone with a crushed toe which was licked by the tongue of a snake and was made whole; one of a man who had come with a spear lodged in his jaw, and by morning the spear was in his hand and his jaw healed; yet another about a man who had only eye sockets, but when dawn came he found he had eyes and could see. Women also came with their fertility problems.

Asclepius' healing powers were such that it was said he even raised a man from the dead. The man was Hippolytus, the son of Theseus whose step-mother, Phaedra, had fallen passionately in love with him, but he had rejected her so she hanged herself, leaving a note accusing him of attempted rape. Theseus did not believe his son when he protested his innocence. Poseidon, god of the sea, who had promised Theseus three wishes, now granted Theseus his wish to be rid of his son; he caused a monster to rise up from the sea and startle the horses pulling Hippolytus' chariot so that he was thrown from it and killed.

When Asclepius brought Hippolytus back to life, Zeus, supreme god of the ancient world, was fearful that Asclepius was overturning the laws of nature so, in order to prevent such a calamity, killed him with a thunderbolt. This enraged Apollo who in his turn killed the Cyclops who had made the thunderbolt. They say that Hippolytus, having been raised from the dead, refused to return to his father's house and ended his days in Italy.

As for the dead Asclepius, well, being the son of Apollo he was semi-divine and, therefore, not really dead. Near to his temple at Epidaurus are now the foundations of what was once a remarkable and magnificent round building known as the Tholos. This some people believe was Asclepius' tomb. The Tholos consisted of a round external Doric colonnade of twenty-six columns supporting a cornice decorated with metopes on which were large rosettes in high relief between triglyphs (grooved panels alternating with the metopes). Inside, it had a circular colonnade of fourteen Corinthian columns, and within that a *cella* with walls of white marble, and windows which let in the light; the floor there was paved with black and white slabs, and at its centre was a movable stone by which people could gain access to a cellar in which were three concentric passages, representing a coiled snake. As a god with Apollo as his father, Asclepius was worshipped in his temple; but, as a hero born of a mortal woman, his power had been gathered from the earth, and he was honoured at the Tholos.

Epidaurus, this remarkable centre of healing, continued

to flourish well into the Christian era. Pagans were not lightly going to turn their backs on a place where miraculous cures had taken place over centuries. In the late fourth century A.D. the Emperor Theodosius I forbade sacrifice, and all but outlawed paganism. In the early fifth century Theodosius II imposed Christianity on the people, and decreed that all pagan temples should be closed down. Two earthquakes in 522 and 551 A.D. caused the final devastation of the great centre.

Little do people realize that for centuries the ancient theatre, which today draws the crowds, was for long concealed under twenty feet of soil. It was only rediscovered in 1870 when a prominent Greek archaeologist, Panagis Kavadias, became convinced of its existence after reading Pausanias' account of his visit to the Asclepeion in the second century A.D. Pausanias wrote that in his opinion no architect could compete with the beauty and harmony of the Epidaurus theatre. Inspired by this, Kavadias excavated the site and brought the theatre back to light. Since 1954 an annual drama festival has been held during the summer months staging the works of the great fifth century dramatists Aeschylus, Euripides, Sophocles and Aristophanes. It is doubtful that those who attend these plays cast their minds back to those early centuries when the sick and disabled spent the night in the *abaton*, trusting in Asclepius to cure them. Today invalids spend the night in a church and depend on a miracle-working icon. Religions might change, but faith and hope remain the same.

* Denotes a separate booklet on the subject.

THE IMMORTAL GODS BORN OF ZEUS BY MORTAL WOMEN

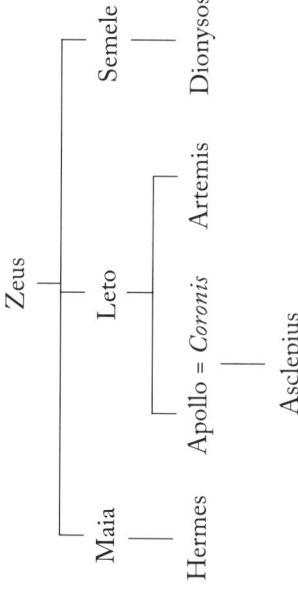

GLOSSARY OF GODS AND GODDESSES

APOLLO – Son of Zeus and the Titaness Leto, twin brother of Artemis. He was god of medicine, music, archery and prophecy. By the mortal woman Coronis he became father of Asclepius.

ARTEMIS – Daughter of Zeus and the Titaness Leto, and twin sister of Apollo. She was goddess of wild life, and defender of the very young, as well as goddess of hunting and archery.

ASCLEPIUS – Son of Apollo and the mortal woman Coronis. He became renowned as a physician and god of healing. He married Epione and had two sons, Machaon and Podalirius, and three daughters, two of whom were Hygiea and Panacea

HYGIEA – Daughter of Asclepius and Epione. The English word 'hygiene' comes from her.

KRONOS – His name is often spelt Cronus (meaning 'time'). He was a Titan and was married to the Titaness Rhea. Poseidon and Zeus were two of their children.

MACHAON – Son of Asclepius and Epione. He was also a doctor and hero who fought in the Trojan War and tended the wounded.

PANACEA – Daughter of Asclepius and Epione, whose name means 'universal remedy'.

PODALIRIUS – Son of Asclepius and Epione. He was mentioned in Homer's Iliad as a physician tending the wounded.

POSEIDON – God of the sea, also of earthquakes and horses. He was often referred to as the 'earth shaker'. He was son of the Titans, Kronos and Rhea, and brother of Zeus.

RHEA – A Titaness, and wife of Kronos. She was mother of Zeus and Poseidon, and other Olympian gods.

TITANS – The offspring of Ouranos (often spelt Uranus, the heavens) and Gaea (the earth). There were said to be twelve of them, six sons and six daughters. Kronos was one of the sons, and Rhea one of the daughters.

MORE FROM THE
PUT IT IN YOUR POCKET SERIES
GREEK MYTHS

TROJAN WAR
THE JUDGEMENT OF PARIS
HELEN
KING AGAMEMNON
ACHILLES
THE WOODEN HORSE
ODYSSEUS

ISLANDS
CHIOS – HOMER
CRETE – THESEUS AND THE MINOTAUR
KOS – HIPPOCRATES AND ASCLEPIUS
NAXOS – THESEUS AND ARIADNE
RHODES – THE COLOSSUS
SANTORINI – THE LOST ISLAND OF ATLANTIS

ALSO BY JILL DUDLEY

YE GODS! (TRAVELS IN GREECE)

YE GODS! II (MORE TRAVELS IN GREECE)

LAP OF THE GODS (TRAVELS IN CRETE
AND THE AEGEAN ISLANDS)

ALSO BY JILL DUDLEY

YE GODS! (TRAVELS IN GREECE)

YE GODS! II (MORE TRAVELS IN GREECE)

LAP OF THE GODS (TRAVELS IN CRETE
AND THE AEGEAN ISLANDS)